Fantastic Cocktails and Mixers

The Confident Cooking Promise of Success

Welcome to the world of Confident Cooking,
where recipes are double-tested by our team
of home economists to achieve a high standard
of success—and delicious results every time.

bay books

C O N T E

Jamaican Coffee, Mexican Coffee, After Dinner Mint, page 104

Boo Boo's Special, Virgin Mary, Limeade, page 102

Illusion, Lord Ashley Cocktail, Frappé, Japanese Slipper, page 60

Russian Roulette Apricot Finale, page 69

Olè, Tequila Sunrise, Strawberry Margarita, Margarita, page 48

The Publisher thanks the following for their assistance in the photography for this book: Accoutrement, Mexico, Noritake, Waterford Wedgwood, Zuhaus.

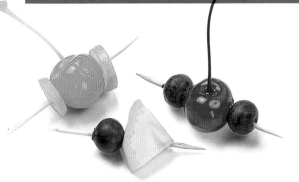

GARNISHES & TOPPINGS

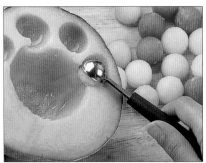

Garnishes do not necessarily have to be eaten, but should always be visually appealing. (Some can even be quite spectacular.) Garnishes will give cocktails colour and shape, and sometimes, even a dash of wit.

Generally, the longer refreshing style of cocktails have more extravagant garnishes that the shorter, stronger cocktails.

FRUITS & VEGETABLES

These simple but effective garnishes can be used on their own, or combined with others to make more elaborate constructions.

Citrus twist: Cut a thin slice of lemon, orange or lime; make a small cut in the slice and twist the slice in opposite directions. Serve on the side of the glass or in the drink. Different coloured citrus fruit can be twisted together and secured with a toothpick. Twists can look effective on toothpicks threaded

between cherries or other small pieces of fruit.

Citrus spiral: Use a vegetable peeler, canelle knife or zester to remove peel in a long continuous strip. The longer the strip, the more it will curl.

Citrus knot: Using strips of peel, carefully tie into a knot.

Melon balls: Use a melon baller and different coloured melons. Thread balls onto toothpicks.

Cartwheels: Using a zester, remove strips of zest straight down from the stalk end at regular intervals to create ridges. (Use these strips for other garnishes.) Slice the fruit; make into twists or pivot on the side of a glass.

Strawberries: Make a small cut in the whole strawberry from base to middle. Nestle on the side of the glass or spear with a cocktail stick and place on the rim of the glass. Make several small cuts in the strawberry and gently spread out to form a fan shape.

Cucumbers: Use a canelle knife or vegetable peeler to remove strips of skin for knotting or curling, slice cucumber into sticks

to stir savoury drinks or make into cartwheels.

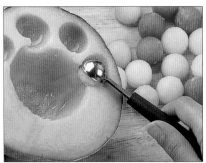

Use a melon baller and different coloured melons.

Fruit pieces can be threaded onto toothpicks.

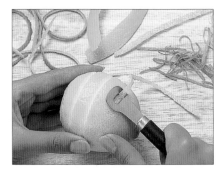

Use a canelle knife (or vegetable peeler) to remove strips of rind.

GRATED TOPPINGS

Use these over drinks containing cream, milk or egg white.

Grate nutmeg directly over the drink.

Use good quality block chocolate at room temperature.

Nutmeg: Use a fresh nutmeg if possible. (Ground nutmeg has a less intense flavour.)
Chocolate: Grate block chocolate over greaseproof paper, then sprinkle on cocktail. For larger flakes, draw a vegetable peeler directly over the edge of the block.
Cinnamon: Use ground form sparingly; it can overpower.

FROSTING

1. Wipe the rim of the glass with a wedge of lemon.
2. Dip the rim in a saucer of either salt or caster (superfine) sugar, press gently and twist to coat. (Sugar can be tinted with grenadine or food colouring for extra effect.)

SKEWERS AND TOOTHPICKS

Thread small wedges of lime, lemon, cumquat, red and green apple, grapes or other colourful small fruits onto toothpicks or small skewers. Alternate and contrast colours with blueberries and small mint leaves, or pieces of pink and white marshmallow and strawberry slices. Thread whole or sliced black or green olives onto toothpicks. Create contrasting shapes with pineapple leaves and melon balls or raspberries, or long wedges of melon or coconut and maraschino cherries or star fruit slices.
Other suggestions: Wrap thin strips of coloured or metallic ribbon around skewers and toothpicks; decorate further with stickers, pipe-cleaners or umbrellas. Toothpicks can be used to join the sweets together.

Thread citrus twists onto toothpicks.

Thinly slice fruit from which peel has been stripped.

Decorate toothpicks with stickers and ribbons.

BAR BASICS

Cocktails are not difficult to make; with a few basic recipes, the right techniques, and imaginative garnishes and glassware you can rival the most elegant cocktail bar.

BAR STOCK

Aim for a variety of cocktail bases that can be adapted to many different types of cocktail. White spirits such as gin, vodka or light rum will blend well with many other (alcoholic and non-alcoholic) ingredients, and are used in both sweet and savoury drinks. Brown spirits, such as scotch and brandy, can be drunk neat—without a mixer— or made into cocktails. Remember that they will affect the colour of the drink. Liqueurs are always sweet, and flavoured with fruit, herbs or nuts, some of them quite strongly. Liqueurs are less adaptable than spirits, although

they do make the most delicious and memorable drinks. As well as alcohol bases, you will need mixers, such as fruit juices and carbonated drinks, garnishes (see pages 4 and 5 for ideas) and plenty of ice.

ICE

Almost all cocktails are served or prepared with ice. (The exceptions are champagne cocktails—which are too volatile—and shooters' and layered drinks which are usually served at room temperature.)

Use cubed ice unless otherwise specified. Small cubes melt quickly, so are ideal for shaken drinks. Where any recipes require crushed ice, allow ice cubes to thaw slightly, then place

in a blender or wrap the ice in a tea-towel and crush with a hammer. If preparing large fruity drinks, such as punches, consider freezing pieces of fruit, or mint leaves, in the ice cubes, or freezing flat liquids other than water, such as cordials, fruit juice or tea.

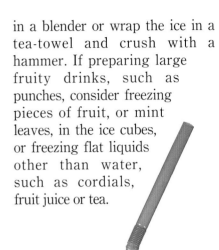

Brandy balloon   *Champagne saucer*   *Liqueur coffee glass*   *Highball glass*

SUGAR SYRUP

Many cocktails require this ingredient. Combine equal parts water and sugar in a saucepan. Stir to dissolve sugar. Bring to boil, reduce heat and simmer until liquid has reduced by half. Allow to cool and refrigerate.

EQUIPMENT

Perhaps the only indispensable item for making cocktails is the **cocktail shaker.** It consists of two pieces which overlap when fitted together. Secure the second piece over the first and shake vigorously to mix the cocktail.

Other useful pieces of equipment would include: a blender or food processor, tongs, teaspoons, a chopping board and knife, corkscrew, metal strainer, mixing jug with stirrer, cocktail sticks, swizzle sticks and straws.

GLASSES

These are illustrated below. Use glasses that are appropriate to the style of drink. For example, strong short cocktails, such as a daiquiri or whisky sour, should be served in a small glass, such as a martini glass or tumbler. Long drinks containing non-alcoholic mixers such as fruit juices or soft drinks, should be served in a highball glass or large goblet. Glasses should be clean and free from detergent smear. Polish glasses with a tea-towel, if necessary.

TECHNIQUES

Shake: Half-fill a cocktail shaker with ice, then add liquid ingredients; shake vigorously. Strain the contents before serving.
Stir: In a jug or serving glass, pour ingredients over ice and stir gently with glass stirrer or long-handled spoon.
Build: Prepare directly in serving glass. Either pour the ingredients over crushed ice, or layer the ingredients one on top of the other. (this may take some practice).
Note: All the recipes in this book serve one, unless otherwise stated. Quantities are given in standard mls and bar measures. Each bar measure contains 30 ml (or 1 fl oz). A 30 ml bar measure can be bought from liquor outlets. However any sort of vessel—a medicine glass, even the screwtop lid from a liquor bottle—can be used. Quantities can be altered according to need, but proportions should remain the same. Pictured garnishes and suggestions for glassware are a guide only. Your imagination is your most important ingredient.

Large goblet   *Champagne flute*   *Martini glass*   *Tumbler*

FINGER FOOD

MUSTARD BEEF TOASTS

Combine 4 tablespoons sour cream, 1–2 teaspoons hot English mustard and 2 teaspoons finely chopped chives in a small bowl. Spoon a little of the cream mixture over 20 mini melba toasts. Top each with a piece of thinly sliced rare roast beef. Garnish with extra chopped chives and finely shredded lemon zest. Makes 20

CHEESE AND ONION PASTRIES

Combine 35 g (1/4 cup) crumbled feta cheese, 1–2 finely chopped spring onions (scallions), 25 g (1/4 cup) grated fresh parmesan cheese, 2 tablespoons finely crumbled blue cheese and black pepper, to taste. Brush 2 sheets filo pastry with melted butter or oil. Top each sheet with another sheet of pastry and brush with a little more butter. Cut pastry sheets into quarters, then into quarters again. Place 1/2 teaspoon of cheese mixture along one edge of each pastry square. Roll up in a cigar shape and pinch the ends to seal. Place pastries on baking tray; sprinkle with extra pepper and bake in preheated 180°C (350°F/ Gas 4) oven 5–10 minutes or until golden and crisp. Serve immediately. Makes 16

TERIYAKI CHICKEN BITES

Combine 60 ml (1/4 cup) soy sauce, 1 tablespoon honey, 1 clove crushed garlic, 1 teaspoon fresh grated ginger and 2 teaspoons sweet sherry in medium bowl. Cut 4 chicken breast or thigh fillets into 2 cm (3/4 inch) cubes and add to marinade. Cover and refrigerate several hours or overnight. Heat 1–2 tablespoons each of sesame oil and olive oil in large frying pan. Cook chicken pieces in batches over medium heat until browned and cooked through. Skewer with toothpicks and serve hot with sweet chilli sauce for dipping. Makes about 20

TOMATO AND OLIVE PASTRIES

Brush 4 sheets ready-rolled puff pastry with melted butter or oil. Spread 2 sheets thinly with sun-dried tomato paste. Spread remaining 2 sheets with olive paste. Cut each sheet into squares or triangles. Top tomato pastry with finely sliced prosciutto or ham, finely sliced red onion rings and 40 g (1/3 cup) grated cheddar cheese. Top the olive pastry with thinly sliced red and green capsicum (pepper) strips, fresh oregano leaves and

Mustard Beef Toasts

Cheese and Onion Pastries

Teriyaki Chicken Bites

Tomato and Olive Pastries

50 g (^{1}/$_3$ cup) grated mozzarella or crumbled feta cheese. Place pastries on greased oven trays. Bake in preheated moderately hot 200°C (400°F/Gas 6) oven for 10–15 minutes or until crisp. Serve hot or warm. Garnish with fresh herbs, if desired.
Makes 32

AVOCADO ROUNDS

Using electric beaters, beat 100 g (3^1/$_2$ oz) cream cheese until soft. Add ^{1}/$_2$ large mashed avocado, 2 tablespoons sour cream, 2–3 teaspoons lemon juice, 1–2 tablespoons finely chopped coriander (cilantro), ^{1}/$_2$ teaspoon ground cumin and salt and pepper, to taste. Beat until mixture is smooth and creamy. Spoon or pipe mixture onto pumpernickel rounds. Top with finely sliced smoked salmon and extra coriander leaves, if desired. Serve immediately.
Makes about 30

BAKED HERB AND CHEESE CUBES

Remove crusts from a whole loaf of unsliced white or wholegrain bread. Cut bread into 2 cm (^{3}/$_4$ inch) cubes. Combine 2 eggs, 15 g (^{1}/$_2$ oz) melted butter, 2 teaspoons each finely chopped parsley and thyme, salt, black pepper and Tabasco sauce or cayenne pepper (to taste) in a small bowl. Whisk until well combined. Dip the bread cubes in the egg mixture and roll in combined 90 g (^{3}/$_4$ cup) grated cheddar cheese and 50 g (^{1}/$_2$ cup) finely grated parmesan cheese. Place on a tray; cover and refrigerate

Avocado Rounds

Baked Herb and Cheese Cubes

several hours or overnight. Place cubes on an oven tray lined with baking paper. Bake in preheated 180°C (350°F/Gas 4) oven 8–10 minutes or until golden and slightly crusty. Serve hot. Sprinkle with ground paprika before baking, if desired.
Makes about 50

CAVIAR OYSTERS

Remove any grit from 1–2 dozen fresh oysters in the shell. Spoon over ^{1}/$_2$-1 teaspoon sour cream, crème fraîche or seafood sauce. Top with red and black caviar and a sprig of dill or lemon thyme. Serve. Add 1–2 cloves freshly crushed garlic and salt and pepper (to taste) to sour cream before spooning over oysters.
Makes 1–2 dozen

TOMATO AND CHEESE TOASTS

Cut a large French bread stick into 2 cm (^{3}/$_4$ inch) slices. Place bread slices on oven tray. Bake in preheated 180°C (350°F/Gas 4) oven 10–15 minutes or until both sides lightly golden. Spread each slice with ^{1}/$_2$-1 teaspoon of sun-dried tomato paste or olive paste. Top each slice with a thin slice of tomato. Finely slice 4–5 bocconcini. Place on top of tomato. Place under preheated grill 1–3 minutes or until cheese begins to soften. Sprinkle with shredded fresh basil leaves. Serve warm.
Makes about 10–15

Caviar Oysters

Tomato and Cheese Toasts

HIGHLY SPIRITED

RUM

Daiquiri

ice
45 ml (1¹/₂ measures)
   light rum
30 ml (1 measure) lemon juice
30 ml (1 measure) Cointreau
15 ml (¹/₂ measure)
   sugar syrup

Place ice, rum, lemon juice, Cointreau and sugar syrup in shaker; shake well. Strain into a martini glass.

Strawberry Daiquiri

crushed ice
45 ml (1¹/₂ measures)
   light rum
30 ml (1 measure) Cointreau
15 ml (¹/₂ measure)
   strawberry liqueur
30 ml (1 measure) lime juice
4 fresh strawberries

Place ice, rum, Cointreau, liqueur, lime juice and strawberries in blender. Blend until well mixed. Pour into a large goblet. Serve with a straw.

Kings Daiquiri

crushed ice
45 ml (1¹/₂ measures)
   light rum
15 ml (¹/₂ measure)
   Parfait Amour
15 ml (¹/₂ measure)
   lemon juice
¹/₄ teaspoon sugar
dash egg white

Place ice, rum, Parfait Amour, juice, sugar and egg white in a blender. Blend until well mixed. Pour into a champagne flute.

Frozen Mango Daiquiri

crushed ice
45 ml (1¹/₂ measures)
   light rum
30 ml (1 measure) Cointreau
15 ml (¹/₂ measure)
   mango liqueur
30 ml (1 measure) lemon juice
pulp of 1 mango

Place ice, rum, Cointreau, liqueur, lemon juice and mango pulp in blender. Blend until well mixed. Pour into a large goblet.

Left to right: Daiquiri, Strawberry Daiquiri, Frozen Mango Daiquiri, Kings Daiquiri

Mai Tai

crushed ice
60 ml (2 measures) light rum
30 ml (1 measure) dark rum
15 ml (½ measure) Cointreau
15 ml (½ measure) Amaretto
15 ml (½ measure)
   lemon juice
90 ml (3 measures)
   pineapple juice
90 ml (3 measures)
   orange juice
15 ml (½ measure)
   sugar syrup
dash grenadine

Half fill a goblet with crushed ice. Add light rum, dark rum, Cointreau, Amaretto, lemon juice, pineapple juice, orange juice, sugar syrup and grenadine. Stir with a swizzle stick.

Pina Colada

crushed ice
45 ml (1½ measures)
   light rum
30 ml (1 measure)
   coconut cream
30 ml (1 measure)
   Malibu liqueur
90 ml (3 measures)
   pineapple juice

Place ice, rum, coconut cream, Malibu and pineapple juice in a blender; blend well. Strain into a tall goblet. Serve with a straw.

Fluffy Duck

ice
30 ml (1 measure) light rum
30 ml (1 measure) Advocaat
15 ml (½ measure) Cointreau
30 ml (1 measure)
   orange juice
30 ml (1 measure) cream
30 ml (1 measure) lemonade

Place ice, rum, Advocaat, Cointreau, orange juice and cream in a cocktail shaker: shake well. Strain into a large martini glass and top with lemonade.

Envy

ice
30 ml (1 measure) light rum
15 ml (½ measure) Amaretto
15 ml (½ measure)
   blue curaçao
15 ml (½ measure) lime juice
75 ml (2½ measures)
   pineapple juice

Place ice, rum, Amaretto, blue curaçao, lime juice and pineapple juice in cocktail shaker; shake well. Strain into a highball glass.

Left to right: Pina Colada, Mai Tai, Fluffy Duck, Envy

Between the Sheets

ice
30 ml (1 measure) light rum
30 ml (1 measure) brandy
30 ml (1 measure) Cointreau
dash lemon juice

Place ice, rum, brandy, Cointreau and lemon juice in cocktail shaker; shake well. Strain into a martini glass. Decorate with a small flower, if desired.

Banana Cow

Crème de banane is a sweet banana-flavoured liqueur which comes in white or yellow varieties. Use white liqueur in this recipe for best results.

ice
30 ml (1 measure) light rum
30 ml (1 measure)
    crème de banane
45 ml (1½ measures) cream
dash grenadine

Place ice, rum, crème de banane, cream and grenadine in shaker; shake together well. Strain into a champagne saucer.

Long Island Iced Tea

crushed ice
15 ml (½ measure) light rum
15 ml (½ measure) vodka
15 ml (½ measure) gin
15 ml (½ measure) Cointreau
15 ml (½ measure) tequila
cola
dash lemon juice

Place ice, rum, vodka, gin, Cointreau and tequila in tall glass; top with cola and lemon juice.

Long Island Lizard

crushed ice
15 ml (½ measure) light rum
15 ml (½ measure) gin
15 ml (½ measure) Cointreau
60 ml (2 measures)
    lemon juice
90 ml (3 measures) lemonade
15 ml (½ measure) Midori
15 ml (½ measure)
    blue curaçao

Place ice in a tall goblet. Add rum, gin, Cointreau, lemon juice and lemonade, then Midori and blue curaçao. Stir with a swizzle stick and serve with a straw.

Left to right: Banana Cow, Long Island Iced Tea, Between the Sheets, Long Island Lizard

IRISH WHISKEY

Dublin Milkshake

ice
45 ml (1½ measures)
    Irish whiskey
30 ml (1 measure) Baileys
120 ml (4 measures)
    cold milk
1 scoop vanilla ice-cream
1 teaspoon powdered
    drinking chocolate

Place ice, whiskey, Baileys and milk in cocktail shaker; shake well. Pour into highball glass. Top with ice-cream and dust with chocolate.

Emerald Isle

ice
45 ml (1½ measures)
    Irish whiskey
30 ml (1 measure) Midori
cold water

Place ice, whiskey and Midori in highball glass; stir well. Top with water.

Golden Gate

ice
30 ml (1 measure)
    Irish whiskey
30 ml (1 measure) Cointreau
15 ml (½ measure)
    orange cordial
dash egg white
dash Pernod

Place ice, whiskey, Cointreau, cordial, egg white and Pernod in cocktail shaker; shake well. Pour into martini glass.

CANADIAN WHISKY

Manhattan (dry)

ice
45 ml (1$\frac{1}{2}$ measures)
  Canadian whisky
15 ml ($\frac{1}{2}$ measure)
  dry vermouth
dash bitters

Place ice, whisky, vermouth and bitters in mixing jug; stir gently to combine. Pour into martini glass.

New York Cocktail

ice
45 ml (1$\frac{1}{2}$ measures)
  Canadian whisky
5 ml (1 teaspoon) lime juice
dash grenadine

Place ice, whisky, juice and grenadine in cocktail shaker; shake well. Pour into tumbler.

King Edward Cocktail

ice
45 ml (1$\frac{1}{2}$ measures)
  Canadian whisky
dash Pernod
dash vermouth
dash water

Stir ice, whisky, Pernod, vermouth and water in mixing jug. Pour into tumbler.

Left to right: Manhattan, King Edward Cocktail, Emerald Isle, Golden Gate, New York Cocktail, Dublin Milkshake

SCOTCH

Use a good quality blended Scotch for mixing these cocktails. Single malt scotch whisky is not generally used to mix cocktails.

Rusty Nail

ice
45 ml (1¹/₂ measures)
    Scotch whisky
45 ml (1¹/₂ measures)
    Drambuie

Half fill a tumbler with ice. Pour over whisky and Drambuie. Stir with a swizzle stick.

Whisky Sour

ice
45 ml (1¹/₂ measures)
    Scotch whisky
30 ml (1 measure) lemon juice
15 ml (¹/₂ measure)
    sugar syrup

Combine ice, whisky, lemon juice and sugar syrup in cocktail shaker; shake well. Strain into tumbler.

Whisky Cobbler

ice
45 ml (1¹/₂ measures)
    Scotch whisky
15 ml (¹/₂ measure) brandy
15 ml (¹/₂ measure)
    white curaçao

Place ice, whisky, brandy and curaçao in goblet; stir to combine.

Whisky Mac

ice
30 ml (1 measure)
    Scotch whisky
30 ml (1 measure) green
    ginger wine
ginger ale

Stir ice, whisky and green ginger wine in mixing jug. Pour into tumbler. Top with ginger ale.

Left to right: Rusty Nail, Whisky Mac, Whisky Sour, Whisky Cobbler

Crazy Horse

ice
30 ml (1 measure)
    Scotch whisky
15 ml (½ measure)
    strawberry liqueur
15 ml (½ measure)
    crème de banane
chilled champagne

Place ice, whisky, strawberry liqueur and crème de banane in cocktail shaker; shake well. Strain into highball glass and top with chilled champagne.

Angel's Kiss

ice
30 ml (1 measure)
    Scotch whisky
30 ml (1 measure)
    sweet vermouth
30 ml (1 measure)
    cherry brandy
30 ml (1 measure)
    orange juice

Place ice, whisky, vermouth, cherry brandy and orange juice in cocktail shaker; shake well. Strain into martini glass.

Left to right: Angel's Kiss, Crazy Horse, Paterson's Curse, Dead 'Orse

Dead 'Orse

ice
30 ml (1 measure)
    Scotch whisky
30 ml (1 measure) lemon juice
1 tablespoon worcestershire
    sauce
1 tablespoon tomato sauce
2 dashes Tabasco sauce
2 dashes bitters
sprinkle of celery salt

Stir ice, whisky, lemon juice,
worcestershire sauce, tomato
sauce, Tabasco sauce and bitters
in mixing jug. Pour into tumbler
and sprinkle lightly with celery
salt.

Paterson's Curse

ice
60 ml (2 measures)
    Scotch whisky
15 ml (1/2 measure)
    crème de cassis
4 dashes orange bitters

Place ice, whisky, crème de cassis
and bitters in cocktail shaker;
shake well. Strain into martini
glass.

Rob Roy

ice
**60 ml (2 measures)
Scotch whisky
30 ml (1 measure)
sweet vermouth
dash bitters**

Combine ice, whisky, vermouth and bitters in a cocktail shaker; shake well. Strain into wine glass.

Old-fashioned Whisky

**1 sugar cube
dash bitters
splash of soda water
ice
60 ml (2 measures)
Scotch whisky**

In a saucer or bowl, soak a sugar cube in bitters until bitters has been absorbed. Place sugar cube in tumbler and top with a good splash of soda water. Add ice and stir to dissolve sugar cube. Add whisky and stir. Serve with a swizzle stick.

Left to right: Bourbon Mint Julep, Rob Roy, Lena Cocktail, Bourbon Mint Julep (in jug), Old-fashioned Whisky

BOURBON

This classic American whisky has a unique taste and should not be replaced with other types of whisky.

Bourbon Mint Julep

ice
60 ml (2 measures) bourbon
4 mint leaves
4 teaspoons sugar
ice, extra
dash dark rum or brandy

Combine ice, bourbon, mint leaves and sugar in a mixing jug; stir. Pour into a highball glass filled with ice and stir gently until glass becomes frosted. Top with a dash of rum or brandy. Serve with a long straw.

Lena Cocktail

30 ml (1 measure) bourbon
15 ml (1/2 measure)
  sweet vermouth
15 ml (1/2 measure)
  dry vermouth
15 ml (1/2 measure) Campari
15 ml (1/2 measure) Galliano
ice

Combine bourbon, sweet vermouth, dry vermouth, Campari and Galliano in a mixing jug filled with ice. Stir gently, then strain into a martini glass.

Burbank Special

ice
60 ml (2 measures) bourbon
60 ml (2 measures)
   orange juice
30 ml (1 measure)
   maple syrup
15 ml ($^1/_2$ measure)
   lemon cordial
1 whole egg

Combine ice, bourbon, orange juice, maple syrup, lemon cordial and egg in cocktail shaker; shake well. Pour slowly into goblet so that froth floats to the top.

French 95

ice
15 ml ($^1/_2$ measure) bourbon
15 ml ($^1/_2$ measure)
   lemon juice
15 ml ($^1/_2$ measure)
   sugar syrup
chilled champagne

Place ice, bourbon, lemon juice and sugar syrup in cocktail shaker; shake well. Pour into champagne flute and top with champagne.

Jim Collins

ice
30 ml (1 measure) bourbon
soda water

Place ice in tumbler. Pour in bourbon and top with soda.

Note: Soda water is best straight from the syphon. If unavailable, use bottled soda water.

Classic Bourbon

ice
45 ml (1$^1/_2$ measures) bourbon
15 ml ($^1/_2$ measure)
   lemon juice
15 ml ($^1/_2$ measure) white
   curaçao
dash Benedictine
dash bitters

Place ice, bourbon, lemon juice, curaçao, Benedictine and bitters in cocktail shaker; shake well. Strain into martini glass. Decorate with flowers, if desired.

Pink Panther

ice
30 ml (1 measure) bourbon
15 ml ($^1/_2$ measure) vodka
30 ml (1 measure)
   coconut milk
15 ml ($^1/_2$ measure) cream
dash grenadine

Place ice, bourbon, vodka, coconut milk, cream and grenadine in cocktail shaker; shake well. Strain into champagne flute.

Left to right: Pink Panther, French 95, Classic Bourbon, Jim Collins, Burbank Special

SOUTHERN COMFORT

Southern Comfort has a bourbon base and is flavoured with peaches.

Comfort Zone

ice
30 ml (1 measure)
  Southern Comfort
30 ml (1 measure) Baileys
60 ml (2 measures) milk
4 strawberries
3 teaspoons sugar syrup

Place ice, Southern Comfort, Baileys, milk, strawberries and sugar syrup in blender; blend until smooth. Pour into highball glass.

Southern Comfort Manhattan

ice
45 ml (1½ measures)
  Southern Comfort
15 ml (½ measure)
  dry vermouth
dash bitters

Combine ice, Southern Comfort, vermouth and bitters in cocktail shaker; shake well. Strain into martini glass.

Riverboat Queen

crushed ice
120 ml (4 measures)
  Southern Comfort
3 teaspoons apricot brandy

Half fill a champagne saucer with crushed ice. Top with Southern Comfort and brandy.

South Seas

ice
30 ml (1 measure)
  Southern Comfort
15 ml (½ measure) Pernod
60 ml (2 measures) orange
  and mango juice
30 ml (1 measure) cream
15 ml (½ measure)
  blue curaçao

Place ice, Southern Comfort, Pernod, juice and cream in cocktail shaker; shake well. Strain into highball glass. Pour blue curaçao slowly through drink so that it sinks to the bottom of the glass.

Tennessee Sour

ice
60 ml (2 measures)
  Southern Comfort
30 ml (1 measure)
  orange curaçao
15 ml (½ measure)
  lemon juice
15 ml (½ measure) lime juice
soda water

Place ice, Southern Comfort, orange curaçao and juices in shaker; shake well. Strain into highball glass. Top with soda water.

Left to right: Comfort Zone, Riverboat Queen, South Seas, Southern Comfort Manhattan, Tennessee Sour

BRANDY

Originally a distilled grape juice, brandy now comes in many forms including fruit-flavoured varieties, such as cherry, apricot and the apple brandy, Calvados. Some recipes in this section use flavoured brandies, but otherwise use a good quality brown brandy.

Brandy Alexander

ice
30 ml (1 measure) brandy
30 ml (1 measure) brown
   crème de cacao
60 ml (2 measures) cream
grated nutmeg

Place ice, brandy, crème de cacao and cream in shaker; shake well. Strain into champagne saucer; sprinkle lightly with nutmeg.

Sidecar

ice
30 ml (1 measure) brandy
20 ml (²/3 measure) Cointreau
5 teaspoons lemon juice

Place ice, brandy, Cointreau and lemon juice in shaker; shake well. Strain into martini glass.

Left to right: Horse's Neck, Sidecar, Brandy Alexander, Brandy, Lime & Soda

Horse's Neck

This drink derives its name from its unusual decoration which resembles a horse' head.

ice
45 ml (1¹/₂ measures) brandy
2 dashes bitters
dry ginger ale
1 lemon, for decoration

Fill a highball glass with ice; pour in brandy, then the bitters. Top with dry ginger ale. Garnish with 'horse' head'
To make horse' head decoration:
Peel away the skin of a lemon in one long piece. Tie a knot in one end. Drape knotted end of peel over the inside edge of a highball glass, so that most of the peel dangles outside the glass.

Brandy, Lime & Soda

ice
30 ml (1 measure) brandy
15 ml (¹/₂ measure) lime juice
dash lime cordial
soda water

Place ice in tumbler; pour in brandy, lime juice and cordial. Top with soda water.

Bosom Caresser

ice
60 ml (2 measures) brandy
30 ml (1 measure)
   orange curaçao
egg yolk
dash grenadine

Place ice, brandy, orange curaçao, egg yolk and grenadine in cocktail shaker; shake well. Strain into martini glass. Decorate with a paper umbrella and simple flower, if desired.

Golden Afternoon

ice
30 ml (1 measure) brandy
15 ml (^{1}/2 measure)
   dry vermouth
15 ml (^{1}/2 measure)
   lime cordial
dry ginger ale

Place ice, brandy, dry vermouth and lime cordial in highball glass. Stir gently to mix and top with dry ginger ale. Serve with straws.

Left to right: Bosom Caresser, Egg Nog, Corpse Reviver, Brandy Orange, Golden Afternoon

Egg Nog

Can also be made with dark rum

**ice
30 ml (1 measure) brandy
30 ml (1 measure) light rum
90 ml (3 measures) milk
3 teaspoons sugar syrup
grated nutmeg**

Place ice, brandy, rum, milk and sugar syrup in blender; blend well. Pour into Irish coffee mug or glass mug. Sprinkle with nutmeg.

Corpse Reviver

**ice
30 ml (1 measure) brandy
15 ml (¹/₂ measure) Calvados
15 ml (¹/₂ measure)
    sweet vermouth**

Place ice, brandy, Calvados and vermouth in cocktail shaker; shake well. Strain into martini glass.

Brandy Orange

**ice
45 ml (1¹/₂ measures) brandy
15 ml (¹/₂ measure)
    orange curaçao
30 ml (1 measure)
    orange juice
dash bitters**

Place ice, brandy, orange curaçao, orange juice and bitters in cocktail shaker; shake well. Strain into champagne saucer.

Cherry Bomb

ice
45 ml (1¹/₂ measures)
    cherry brandy
45 ml (1¹/₂ measures)
    apple cider
dash grenadine
1 teaspoon lemon juice

Combine ice, brandy, apple cider, grenadine and lemon juice in cocktail shaker; shake well. Strain into highball glass.

The Rose

ice
45 ml (1¹/₂ measures)
    apricot brandy
45 ml (1¹/₂ measures) gin
15 ml (¹/₂ measure)
    dry vermouth
dash grenadine

Combine ice, apricot brandy, gin, dry vermouth and grenadine in cocktail shaker; shake well. Strain into martini glass.

B & B

30 ml (1 measure) brandy
30 ml (1 measure) Benedictine

Pour brandy and Benedictine into a warmed brandy balloon.
To warm a brandy balloon:
Pour hot water into the glass, swirl gently for a few moments; discard the water, dry glass and use immediately.

Matilda

ice
30 ml (1 measure) brandy
30 ml (1 measure) Kahlua
30 ml (1 measure) cream
grated nutmeg

Combine ice, brandy, Kahlua and cream in cocktail shaker; shake well. Strain into champagne glass. Sprinkle with nutmeg.

Left to right: Cherry Bomb, Matilda, B & B, The Rose

GIN

Use a good quality London-style dry gin to make these cocktails. Other types of gin include Dutch gin (which is very pungent) and sloe gin, which is flavoured with the fruit of the wild blackthorn. English gin is flavoured with juniper berries and is drier and more subtle than these.

Dry Martini

This is the classic martini, and dry enough for most palates. For an extra-dry martini, add only a dash of vermouth. Some purists will insist that *no* vermouth is used (other than to wash out the glass).

ice
75 ml (2½ measures) gin
15 ml (½ measure)
** dry vermouth**

Combine ice, gin and vermouth in a mixing jug and stir gently. Strain into a martini glass.

Gimlet

ice
45 ml (1½ measure) gin
15 ml (½ measure)
** lime cordial**
long dash soda water

Half fill a large tumbler with ice. Pour in gin and lime cordial. Top with soda water. Stir with a swizzle stick.

Sweet Martini

ice
60 ml (2 measures) gin
30 ml (1 measure)
** sweet vermouth**

Combine ice, gin and sweet vermouth in a mixing jug and stir gently. Strain into a martini glass.

Pink Gin

3 dashes bitters
ice
45 ml (1½ measures) gin
30 ml (1 measure) water

Swirl bitters in a tumbler; shake out excess. Add ice, gin and water. Decorate with an orchid, if desired.

Left to right: Dry Martini, Pink Gin, Sweet Martini, Gimlet

Strawberry Dawn

30 ml (1 measure) gin
30 ml (1 measure)
   coconut cream
2 strawberries
crushed ice

Combine gin, coconut cream, strawberries and plenty of crushed ice in a blender; blend well. Pour into a martini glass.

Gin Sling

ice
45 ml (1½ measures) gin
30 ml (1 measure) lemon juice
dash grenadine
soda water

Place ice in tumbler. Add gin, lemon juice and grenadine; top with soda water.

Left to right: Watermelon Cocktail, Singapore Sling, Strawberry Dawn, Gin Sling

Singapore Sling

ice
60 ml (2 measures) gin
30 ml (1 measure)
    cherry brandy
30 ml (1 measure)
    lemon juice
soda water

Place ice, gin, cherry brandy and lemon juice in shaker; mix well. Strain into highball glass; top with soda water.

Watermelon Cocktail

This unusual cocktail is a delightful summer drink. Watermelon juice cannot be stored, so will need to be prepared just before serving. (You will need only a small slice of peeled watermelon to produce enough juice for this cocktail.)

45 ml (1½ measures) gin
60 ml (2 measures)
    watermelon juice
ice

Combine gin and watermelon juice in an ice-filled jug. Stir and serve in a large goblet.

Gibson

ice
60 ml (2 measures) gin
1 teaspoon dry vermouth

Place ice, gin and vermouth in mixing jug; stir. Pour into martini glass.

White Lady

ice
30 ml (1 measure) gin
15 ml (¹/₂ measure)
    Cointreau
15 ml (¹/₂ measure)
    lemon juice
dash egg white

Combine ice, gin, Cointreau, lemon juice and egg white in martini shaker; shake well. Strain into martini glass. Decorate with a simple flower, if desired.

Sweet 16

crushed ice
30 ml (1 measure) gin
15 ml (¹/₂ measure)
    crème de cacao
15 ml (¹/₂ measure) Malibu
dash coconut cream
30 ml (1 measure)
    pineapple juice

Combine ice, gin, crème de cacao, Malibu, coconut cream and pineapple juice in blender; blend well. Strain into martini glass.

Tom Collins

ice
60 ml (2 measures) gin
60 ml (2 measures)
    lemon juice
15 ml (¹/₂ measure)
    sugar syrup
soda water

Combine ice, gin, lemon juice and sugar syrup in a highball glass; stir well to combine. Top with soda water.

Negroni

ice
30 ml (1 measure) gin
30 ml (1 measure)
    sweet vermouth
30 ml (1 measure) Campari
soda water

Combine ice, gin, vermouth and Campari in highball glass; stir to combine. Top with soda water.

Left to right: Gibson, Sweet 16, Tom Collins, White Lady, Negroni

Fallen Angel

ice
45 ml (1½ measures) gin
15 ml (½ measure) green
  crème de menthe
30 ml (1 measure) lemon juice
dash bitters

Place ice, gin, crème de menthe, lemon juice and bitters in a cocktail shaker; shake well. Strain into a champagne saucer.

Great Barrier Reef

ice
60 ml (2 measures) gin
30 ml (1 measure) Cointreau
dash bitters
dash blue curaçao
2 scoops vanilla ice-cream

Combine ice, gin, Cointreau, bitters, blue curaçao and ice-cream in a blender; blend well. Pour into highball glass.

Left to right: Great Barrier Reef, Harvey Wallbanger, Fallen Angel, Bloody Mary

VODKA

Vodka is an ideal cocktail base as it has no colour or flavour. Vodka will not freeze so can be stored in the freezer indefinitely and brought out when icy-cold cocktails are required.

Bloody Mary

Traditionally, this drink is served with a celery stick to be used as an edible swizzle stick.

crushed ice
dash Tabasco sauce
dash worcestershire sauce
dash lemon juice
salt, to taste
pepper, to taste
60 ml (2 measures) vodka
tomato juice

Place crushed ice in tall goblet. Add Tabasco and worcestershire sauces, lemon juice, salt and pepper; stir well. Pour in vodka, then tomato juice; stir again.

Harvey Wallbanger

crushed ice
30 ml (1 measure) vodka
60 ml (2 measures)
    orange juice
30 ml (1 measure) Galliano

Place crushed ice in large goblet. Pour in vodka and orange juice; stir. Slowly add Galliano by pouring it over the back of a teaspoon. Serve with a straw.

Black Russian

ice
45 ml (1¹/₂ measures) vodka
15 ml (¹/₂ measure) Kahlua

Place ice in tumbler. Add vodka and Kahlua; stir.

White Russian

ice
30 ml (1 measure) vodka
30 ml (1 measure) Kahlua
60 ml (2 measures) milk
grated nutmeg

Place ice in tumbler. Add vodka, Kahlua and milk. Stir with a swizzle stick. Sprinkle with nutmeg.

Salty Dog

salt
ice
45 ml (1¹/₂ measures) vodka
grapefruit juice

Frost the rim of a tumbler with salt (see page 5). Fill glass with ice, add vodka and grapefruit juice; stir gently.

Blue Lagoon

ice
30 ml (1 measure) vodka
15 ml (¹/₂ measure)
   blue curaçao
lemonade

Half fill a highball glass with ice. Add vodka and blue curaçao. Top with lemonade.

Left to right: Blue Lagoon, Salty Dog, White Russian, Black Russian

Chi Chi

crushed ice
45 ml (1¹/₂ measures) vodka
15 ml (¹/₂ measure) Malibu
30 ml (1 measure)
   coconut cream
120 ml (4 measures)
   pineapple juice

Combine ice, vodka, Malibu, coconut cream and pineapple juice in blender; blend well. Pour into large goblet.

Brain Tumour

This aptly named drink is served ungarnished at room temperature, and is, traditionally, drunk in one gulp. Don't be put off by its appearance—this drink is delicious.

15 ml (¹/₂ measure) vodka
15 ml (¹/₂ measure) schnapps
15 ml (¹/₂ measure) Baileys
dash grenadine

Pour vodka, schnapps and Baileys into a liqueur glass. Slowly drizzle grenadine into the glass over the back of a teaspoon.

Left to right: Chi Chi, Brain Tumour, Kamikaze, Screwdriver

Screwdriver

ice
45 ml (1½ measures) vodka
orange juice

Place ice in tumbler. Add vodka and top with orange juice. Serve with a straw.

Kamikaze

ice
30 ml (1 measure) vodka
30 ml (1 measure) Cointreau
30 ml (1 measure) lemon juice
dash lime cordial

Combine ice, vodka, Cointreau, lemon juice and lime cordial in a cocktail shaker; shake well. Strain into martini glass.

Hint

Vodka can be steeped with herbs or fragrant plant products. Try tarragon, honey, chilli, coffee beans, lemon peel or orange peel. Red capsicum (pepper), for example, will turn the vodka pink and give it a peppery flavour.

The flavouring agent should be left in the vodka for at least a week, and stored away from light. Flavoured vodka should not be used as a mixer, but drunk, as it is in Russia, neat and ice-cold.

Electric Iced Tea

ice
30 ml (1 measure) vodka
60 ml (2 measures) cold
    weak black tea
1 teaspoon demerara sugar

Pour ice, vodka, tea and sugar into a highball glass; stir gently until sugar dissolves. Serve with a straw.

Summer Hummer

crushed ice
30 ml (1 measure) vodka
    (from the freezer)
30 ml (1 measure)
    raspberry cordial
60 ml (2 measures) lemonade

Half fill a highball glass with crushed ice. Pour over combined vodka and raspberry cordial. Top with lemonade. Serve with a straw and spoon.

Vodka Martini

ice
45 ml (1½ measures) vodka
15 ml (½ measure)
    dry vermouth

Pour ice, vodka and vermouth in mixing jug; stir gently. Pour into martini glass.

Black Forest

crushed ice
30 ml (1 measure) vodka
    (from the freezer)
30 ml (1 measure) Cointreau
15 ml (½ measure)
    blackberry liqueur
4–5 raspberries
90 ml (3 measures)
    apple juice

Combine ice, vodka, Cointreau, blackberry liqueur, raspberries and apple juice in blender; blend well. Pour into highball glass.

Silver Sunset

ice
30 ml (1 measure) vodka
15 ml (½ measure)
    apricot brandy
15 ml (½ measure) Campari
90 ml (3 measures)
    orange juice
dash egg white

Place ice, vodka, apricot brandy, Campari, orange juice and egg white in cocktail shaker; shake well. Strain into highball glass. Serve with a straw.

Left to right: Black Forest, Silver Sunset, Vodka Martini, Electric Iced Tea, Summer Hummer

TEQUILA

Tequila has a reputation for a high alcohol content, probably due to the original Mexican way of drinking it—a straight shot, accompanied by lemon and salt balanced on the hand (Lick, Sip, Suck). In fact, tequila is no higher in alcohol than gin or rum, and is just as versatile a mixer.

Margarita

salt
ice
45 ml (1^1/$_2$ measures) tequila
15 ml (^{1}/$_2$ measure) Cointreau
30 ml (1 measure) lemon juice

Frost the rim of a martini glass with salt (see page 5). Place ice, tequila, Cointreau and lemon juice in cocktail shaker; shake well and strain into martini glass.

Strawberry Margarita

salt
crushed ice
30 ml (1 measure) tequila
30 ml (1 measure)
    strawberry liqueur
15 ml (^{1}/$_2$ measure) Cointreau
30 ml (1 measure)
    lime cordial
30 ml (1 measure) lemon juice

Frost the rim of a martini glass with salt (see page 5). Place ice, tequila, strawberry liqueur, Cointreau, lime juice cordial and lemon juice in blender; blend well. Pour into martini glass.

Olé

ice
30 ml (1 measure) tequila
30 ml (1 measure)
    banana liqueur
dash blue curaçao

Place ice, tequila and banana liqueur in shaker; shake well. Strain into a liqueur glass. Tip a dash of blue curaçao into the drink to achieve a two-tone effect.

Tequila Sunrise

ice
60 ml (2 measures) tequila
120 ml (4 measures)
    orange juice
dash grenadine

Place ice in highball glass. Add tequila and orange juice, top with grenadine and serve with a swizzle stick.

Left to right: Olé, Tequila Sunrise, Strawberry Margarita, Margarita

Hot Mary

ice
60 ml (2 measures) tequila
15 ml (¹/₂ measure)
   lemon juice
dash worcestershire sauce
2 drops Tabasco sauce
90 ml (3 measures)
   tomato juice
salt and pepper, to taste

Combine ice, tequila, lemon juice, worcestershire sauce, Tabasco sauce and tomato juice in cocktail shaker; shake well. Strain into highball glass. Season to taste.

Freddie Fudputter

ice
45 ml (1¹/₂ measures) tequila
15 ml (¹/₂ measure) Galliano
60 ml (2 measures)
   orange juice

Combine ice, tequila, Galliano and orange juice in cocktail shaker; shake well. Strain into cocktail glass.

Left to right: Hot Mary, Freddie Fudputter, Blue Monday, Kiwi Margarita

Blue Monday

ice
30 ml (1 measure) tequila
30 ml (1 measure) Drambuie
30 ml (1 measure)
   blue curaçao
90 ml (3 measures) lemonade

Combine ice, tequila, Drambuie and blue curaçao in cocktail shaker; shake well. Strain into highball glass. Top with lemonade. Serve with a straw.

Kiwi Margarita

salt for frosting
crushed ice
45 ml (1¹/₂ measures) tequila
30 ml (1 measure) Cointreau
30 ml (1 measure) Midori
30 ml (1 measure) lemon juice
1–2 kiwi fruit, peeled and
   chopped

Frost the rim of a goblet with salt (see page 5). Place ice, tequila, Cointreau, Midori, lemon juice and kiwi fruit in blender; blend well. Pour into goblet.

Brave Bull

ice
30 ml (1 measure) tequila
30 ml (1 measure) Kahlua

Place ice in tumbler. Pour in tequila, then Kahlua; stir gently with a swizzle stick.

Sombrero Spinner

crushed ice
30 ml (1 measure) tequila
30 ml (1 measure) Cointreau
15 ml (1/2 measure)
   strawberry liqueur
45 ml (1 1/2 measures) orange
   and mango juice
4 strawberries

Combine ice, tequila, Cointreau, strawberry liqueur, orange and mango juice and strawberries in blender; blend well. Pour into champagne flute.

Mexican Devil

ice
30 ml (1 measure) tequila
15 ml (1/2 measure)
   crème de cassis
15 ml (1/2 measure) lime juice
dry ginger ale

Half fill highball glass with ice. Pour in tequila, crème de cassis and lime juice; stir gently to combine. Top with dry ginger ale.

Acapulco Gold

ice
30 ml (1 measure) tequila
30 ml (1 measure) Tia Maria
30 ml (1 measure) dark rum
30 ml (1 measure)
   pineapple juice
30 ml (1 measure)
   coconut cream

Combine ice, tequila, Tia Maria, dark rum, juice and coconut cream in cocktail shaker; shake well. Strain into highball glass.

The Myths about Tequila

As mentioned in the introduction to this section, tequila is no more potent than gin or rum, nor is it related to the hallucinatory drug, mescaline. Tequila is made from the juice of the agave plant, also known as *mezcal* in some parts of Mexico. Thus, the term for inferior grades of tequila, 'mezcal' has become confused with the similar-sounding mescaline and spawned legends about blindness, madness and vision-inducing worms. A few bottlers of tequila do drop a worm from the mezcal plant into their finished product, however there is no truth to the rumour that eating it will cause hallucinations, extreme inebriation, or anything other than indigestion.

Left to right: Mexican Devil, Sombrero Spinner, Acapulco Gold, Brave Bull

PIMM'S

Originally in six varieties (with different spirit bases) and one of the earliest cocktail mixers, Pimm's is still a popular cocktail base.

Pimm's No. 1

This is the original Pimm's cocktail, traditionally enjoyed after a round of golf or a game of tennis.

ice
60 ml (2 measures)
    Pimm's No. 1
90 ml (3 measures) lemonade
90 ml (3 measures) dry
    ginger ale

Half fill a highball glass with ice cubes. Pour over Pimm's, lemonade and ginger ale. Stir with a swizzle stick and serve with a straw.

Note: When champagne is used in place of the lemonade and ginger ale, the drink is known as a Pimm's Royal—another classic drink.

Left to right: Golden Glove, Pimm's Spritz, Pimm's No. 1, Pimm's Reef

Pimm's Reef

ice
30 ml (1 measure)
    Pimm's No. 1
15 ml (¹/2 measure)
    blue curaçao
30 ml (1 measure) cream

Combine ice, Pimm's, blue curaçao and cream in cocktail shaker; shake well. Strain into martini glass.

Golden Glove

ice
30 ml (1 measure)
    Pimm's No. 1
15 ml (¹/2 measure) Amaretto
15 ml (¹/2 measure) Galliano
lemonade

Combine ice, Pimm's, Amaretto and Galliano in cocktail shaker; shake well. Strain into highball glass. Top with lemonade.

Pimm's Spritz

ice
30 ml (1 measure)
    Pimm's No. 1
30 ml (1 measure) gin
90 ml (3 measures) lemonade

Half fill a goblet with ice. Pour over Pimm's, gin and lemonade. Stir with a swizzle stick.

LUSCIOUS LIQUEURS

MIDORI

One of many popular mixers flavoured with fruit, Midori has the flavour and hue of the honeydew melon.

Midori Splice

crushed ice
30 ml (1 measure) Midori
30 ml (1 measure) Cointreau
15 ml (½ measure) Malibu
90 ml (3 measures)
    pineapple juice
60 ml (2 measures) cream

Combine ice, Midori, Cointreau, Malibu, pineapple juice and cream in blender; blend well. Pour into large goblet. Serve with a straw.

Japanese Traffic Lights

30 ml (1 measure)
    banana liqueur
30 ml (1 measure)
    strawberry liqueur
30 ml (1 measure) Midori

Pour banana liqueur into martini glass. Slowly pour over strawberry liqueur, then Midori to form three distinct layers.

Melon Sour

ice
30 ml (1 measure) Midori
60 ml (2 measures)
    lemon juice
dash egg white

Combine ice, Midori, lemon juice and egg white in cocktail shaker; shake well. Strain into goblet.

Shady Lady

ice
30 ml (1 measure) Midori
30 ml (1 measure) tequila
90 ml (3 measures)
    grapefruit juice

Combine ice, Midori, tequila and grapefruit juice in cocktail shaker; shake well. Strain and pour into goblet.

Left to right: Midori Splice, Japanese Traffic Lights, Melon Sour, Shady Lady

Twice as Nice

ice
30 ml (1 measure) Midori
15 ml (1/2 measure) light rum
30 ml (1 measure) Malibu
30 ml (1 measure) cream
60 ml (2 measures)
    pineapple juice

Combine ice, Midori, rum, Malibu, cream and pineapple juice in a cocktail shaker; shake well. Strain into a champagne saucer.

Embryo

15 ml (1/2 measure) Midori
15 ml (1/2 measure) Baileys
15 ml (1/2 measure) Advocaat

Pour Midori into liqueur glass. Slowly pour Baileys, then Advocaat over Midori, to create a two-layered effect.

Left to right: Twice as Nice, Tropicana, Fruit Tingle, Embryo

Fruit Tingle

crushed ice
30 ml (1 measure) Midori
30 ml (1 measure) Cointreau
30 ml (1 measure)
   blue curaçao
90 ml (3 measures)
   pineapple juice
dash lemon juice
dash grenadine

Place ice, Midori, Cointreau, blue curaçao, pineapple juice, lemon juice and grenadine in a blender; blend well. Strain into large goblet. Serve with a straw.

Tropicana

ice
15 ml (¹/₂ measure) Midori
15 ml (¹/₂ measure) Malibu
15 ml (¹/₂ measure) Cointreau
45 ml (1¹/₂ measures)
   pineapple juice
lemonade

Combine ice, Midori, Malibu, Cointreau and pineapple juice in a cocktail shaker. Strain into a tall goblet. Top with lemonade.

Japanese Slipper

ice
30 ml (1 measure) Midori
30 ml (1 measure) Cointreau
lemon juice

Combine ice, Midori, Cointreau and lemon juice in a cocktail shaker; shake well. Strain and serve in a chilled martini glass.

Illusion

ice
15 ml (¹/₂ measure) Midori
15 ml (¹/₂ measure) Cointreau
30 ml (1 measure) Malibu
30 ml (1 measure) cream

Combine ice, Midori, Cointreau, Malibu and cream in cocktail shaker; shake well. Strain into champagne saucer.

Left to right: Illusion, Lord Ashley Cocktail, Frappé, Japanese Slipper

COINTREAU

Cointreau is the best known of the triple sec liqueurs. It is colourless and subtly flavoured with oranges. While it is often enjoyed on its own over crushed ice, its sweetness makes it a popular mixer in many cocktails and party drinks.

Lord Ashley Cocktail

ice
15 ml (1/2 measure) Cointreau
15 ml (1/2 measure) Advocaat
15 ml (1/2 measure) white
  crème de cacao
15 ml (1/2 measure)
  crème de banane
30 ml (1 measure) cream

Place ice, Cointreau, Advocaat, crème de cacao, crème de banane and cream in a cocktail shaker; shake well. Strain into a goblet.

Frappé

Frappés can be made with any liqueur or liqueur combination. Simply pour over crushed ice. The frappé is usually served with a long-handled spoon.

crushed ice
15 ml (1/2 measure) Cointreau
30 ml (1 measure)
  Parfait Amour

Fill a large brandy balloon with crushed ice. Pour over Cointreau, then Parfait Amour. Stir gently with a swizzle stick. Decorate with violets, if desired.

Life Saver

ice
30 ml (1 measure) Cointreau
15 ml (½ measure) brandy
15 ml (½ measure)
    grapefruit juice
15 ml (½ measure) white
    crème de menthe
tonic water

Combine ice, Cointreau, brandy, grapefruit juice and white crème de menthe in cocktail shaker; shake well. Strain into goblet. Top with tonic water.

Per F'Amour

ice
30 ml (1 measure) Cointreau
15 ml (½ measure)
    Parfait Amour
45 ml (1½ measures)
    orange juice
dash egg white

Combine ice, Cointreau, Parfait Amour, orange juice and dash of egg white in shaker; shake well. Strain into champagne saucer. Decorate with several rose petals, if desired.

Banana Bender

ice
30 ml (1 measure) Cointreau
30 ml (1 measure)
    banana liqueur
60 ml (2 measures) cream
1 banana, peeled and sliced

Combine ice, Cointreau, banana liqueur, cream and banana in blender; blend well. Pour into champagne glass.

Strawberry Daze

crushed ice
30 ml (1 measure) Cointreau
15 ml ($\frac{1}{2}$ measure) tequila
15 ml ($\frac{1}{2}$ measure)
  strawberry liqueur
45 ml ($1\frac{1}{2}$ measures)
  orange juice
4 strawberries

Combine crushed ice, Cointreau, tequila, strawberry liqueur, orange juice and strawberries in blender; blend well. Pour into goblet. Serve with a straw.

Japanese Egg Nog

ice
45 ml ($1\frac{1}{2}$ measures)
  Cointreau
45 ml ($1\frac{1}{2}$ measures) Midori
90 ml (3 measures) milk
dash egg white

Combine ice, Cointreau, Midori, milk and egg white in cocktail shaker; shake well. Strain into martini glass.

Left to right: Japanese Egg Nog, Life Saver, Strawberry Daze, Per F'Amour, Banana Bender

MALIBU

Malibu is a sweet, rum-based liqueur, flavoured with coconut, that blends well with other sweet liqueurs and exotic or tropical fruits.

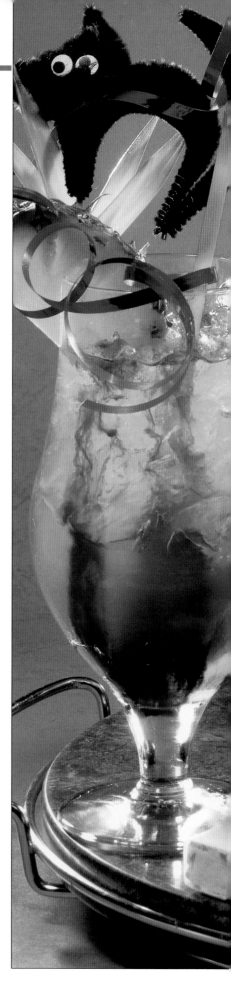

Happy Days

ice
30 ml (1 measure) Malibu
30 ml (1 measure)
    peach schnapps
15 ml (½ measure) Advocaat
60 ml (2 measures)
    orange juice
60 ml (2 measures)
    pineapple juice
60 ml (2 measures) cream

Place ice, Malibu, schnapps, Advocaat, juices and cream in cocktail shaker; shake well. Strain into martini glass.

Copacabana

ice
15 ml (½ measure) Malibu
15 ml (½ measure)
    crème de banane
15 ml (½ measure)
    Grand Marnier
60 ml (2 measures)
    pineapple juice
30 ml (1 measure)
    coconut cream

Combine ice, Malibu, crème de banane, Grand Marnier, pineapple juice and coconut cream in cocktail shaker; shake well. Strain into champagne saucer.

Poison

crushed ice
30 ml (1 measure) Malibu
30 ml (1 measure) Midori
15 ml (½ measure)
    blue curaçao
90 ml (3 measures)
    pineapple juice
dash lemon juice
champagne
dash grenadine

Fill a large goblet with ice. Pour over Malibu, Midori, blue curaçao, and pineapple and lemon juices. Top with champagne and a dash of grenadine.

Tropical Night

ice
30 ml (1 measure) Malibu
30 ml (1 measure) Midori
15 ml (½ measure)
    lemon juice
15 ml (½ measure) lime juice

Combine ice, Malibu, Midori, lemon and lime juice in cocktail shaker; shake well. Strain into martini glass.

Left to right: Poison, Happy Days, Tropical Night, Copacabana

GALLIANO

This Italian liqueur, which comes in the distinctive cone-shaped bottle, is flavoured with aniseed.

Golden Dream

ice
30 ml (1 measure) Galliano
15 ml (1/2 measure) Cointreau
15 ml (1/2 measure)
    orange juice
15 ml (1/2 measure) cream

Combine ice, Galliano, Cointreau, orange juice and cream in a cocktail shaker; shake well. Strain into martini glass.

Ewok Attack

crushed ice
15 ml (1/2 measure) Galliano
15 ml (1/2 measure)
    apricot brandy
15 ml (1/2 measure) Midori
15 ml (1/2 measure) light rum
15 ml (1/2 measure) tequila
90 ml (3 measures)
    orange juice
90 ml (3 measures)
    pineapple juice

Half fill a large goblet with crushed ice. Pour over Galliano, apricot brandy, Midori, rum, tequila, orange juice and pineapple juice.

Fellini

ice
45 ml (1 1/2 measures) Galliano
30 ml (1 measure) Frangelico
30 ml (1 measure) lemon juice

Combine ice, Galliano, Frangelico, and lemon juice in a cocktail shaker; shake well. Strain into martini glass.

Screaming Orgasm

ice
30 ml (1 measure) Galliano
30 ml (1 measure) Baileys
15 ml (1/2 measure) Cointreau
15 ml (1/2 measure) Kahlua
30 ml (1 measure) cream

Combine ice, Galliano, Baileys, Cointreau, Kahlua and cream in a cocktail shaker; shake well. Strain into a martini glass.

Left to right: Screaming Orgasm, Ewok Attack, Fellini, Golden Dream

Rockmelon Dream

crushed ice
30 ml (1 measure) Galliano
15 ml (¹/₂ measure)
    maraschino liqueur
30 ml (1 measure)
    orange juice
30 ml (1 measure) cream
¹/₄ rockmelon, peeled and
    chopped

Combine ice, Galliano, maraschino liqueur, orange juice, cream and rockmelon pieces in blender; blend well. Pour into champagne saucer.

The Impossible Dream

This is a layered drink, an effect not easy to achieve—the secret is gentle pouring and a steady hand, so perhaps try this one at the beginning of the evening.

1 teaspoon Galliano
30 ml (1 measure) light rum
15 ml (¹/₂ measure)
    blue curaçao
15 ml (¹/₂ measure) Advocaat
15 ml (¹/₂ measure)
    cherry liqueur
15 ml (¹/₂ measure)
    yellow chartreuse
15 ml (¹/₂ measure)
    green chartreuse

Pour Galliano into champagne flute, followed by the rum, blue curaçao, Advocaat, cherry liqueur, yellow chartreuse and green chartreuse, so they form layers.

Left to right: Lamborghini, Impossible Dream, Rockmelon Dream, Russian Roulette, Apricot Finale

Russian Roulette

crushed ice
15 ml (¹/₂ measure) Galliano
15 ml (¹/₂ measure) vodka
15 ml (¹/₂ measure)
  banana liqueur
15 ml (¹/₂ measure)
  lemon juice
1 teaspoon sugar syrup
¹/₂ banana, peeled and sliced

Combine ice, Galliano, vodka, banana liqueur, lemon juice, sugar syrup and banana in blender; blend well. Pour into highball glass. Serve with a straw.

Apricot Finale

ice
30 ml (1 measure) Galliano
30 ml (1 measure)
  apricot brandy
60 ml (2 measures)
  apricot juice
2 scoops ice-cream, slightly
  softened

Combine ice, Galliano, apricot brandy, apricot juice and ice-cream in cocktail shaker; shake well. Strain into goblet.

Lamborghini

15 ml (¹/₂ measure) Kahlua
15 ml (¹/₂ measure) Galliano
15 ml (¹/₂ measure)
  green chartreuse

Pour Kahlua into port or sherry glass, followed by Galliano, then green chartreuse.

Note: A Flaming Lamborghini is made as above; the top is set on fire, very briefly, before drinking.

BAILEYS

This smooth, chocolate-flavoured liqueur has an Irish whiskey base and blends well with milk or cream.

Murder on the Orient Express

ice
45 ml (1½ measures) Baileys
45 ml (1½ measures)
　chilled vodka
30 ml (1 measure) Frangelico
dash white crème de cacao

Combine ice, Baileys, vodka, Frangelico in cocktail shaker; shake well. Strain into liqueur glass. Top with white crème de cacao.

Monkey's Lunch

ice
30 ml (1 measure) Baileys
30 ml (1 measure)
　crème de banane
30 ml (1 measure) Malibu
15 ml (½ measure) cream

Combine ice, Baileys, crème de banane, Malibu and cream in cocktail shaker; shake well. Strain into highball glass. Serve with a straw.

Matterhorn

crushed ice
30 ml (1 measure) Baileys
30 ml (1 measure) Kahlua
15 ml (½ measure)
　crème de banane

Fill a large goblet with crushed ice. Pour over Baileys, Kahlua and crème de banane. Do not stir.

Angel

ice
30 ml (1 measure) Baileys
15 ml (½ measure) Cointreau
15 ml (½ measure)
　strawberry liqueur
30 ml (1 measure)
　pineapple juice
30 ml (1 measure) cream
4 strawberries

Combine ice, Baileys, Cointreau, strawberry liqueur, pineapple juice, cream and strawberries in a blender; mix well. Pour into a large goblet.

Left to right: Murder on the Orient Express, Monkey's Lunch, Angel, Matterhorn

Orgasm

ice
30 ml (1 measure) Baileys
30 ml (1 measure) Cointreau

Place ice in tumbler. Pour over Baileys, then Cointreau.

Baileys Smoothie

ice
30 ml (1 measure) Baileys
15 ml (¹/₂ measure) Kahlua
15 ml (¹/₂ measure) Advocaat
60 ml (2 measures) cream
1 banana, peeled and sliced

Combine ice, Baileys, Kahlua, Advocaat, cream and banana in a blender; blend well. Serve in a large goblet with a straw.

Hints

Try a nip of Baileys in Irish coffee or to make an adult milkshake. A tablespoon of Baileys can be used as a topping for ice-cream, a chocolate-based trifle or used to freshen up a stale cake.

To make Irish liqueur cream: Place 375 ml (1¹/₂ cups) condensed milk, 300 ml (1¹/₄ cups) cream, 250 ml (1 cup) Irish whiskey, ¹/₄ tablespoon vanilla essence, 2 tablespoons chocolate topping and 3 eggs, in a blender. Process mixture for 20–30 seconds or until it just begins to thicken.
Serves 6–8
Store in refrigerator 2–3 weeks.

KAHLUA

This sweet, dark liqueur is made with coffee beans, cocoa beans, vanilla and brandy. It is sometimes served, neat with ice, as an after-dinner drink.

KGB

30 ml (1 measure) Kahlua
30 ml (1 measure) Baileys
30 ml (1 measure)
  Grand Marnier

Pour Kahlua, then Baileys and finally Grand Marnier into a shot glass. Do not stir or mix. Ingredients should form three layers.

Seduction

30 ml (1 measure) Kahlua
30 ml (1 measure) Midori
30 ml (1 measure) Baileys

Pour Kahlua, then Midori and finally Baileys into a shot glass. Do not stir or mix. Ingredients should form three layers.

Left to right: Baileys Smoothie, KGB, Seduction, Orgasm

Heaven

crushed ice
15 ml (¹/₂ measure) Kahlua
15 ml (¹/₂ measure)
    brown crème de cacao
15 ml (¹/₂ measure) Baileys
15 ml (¹/₂ measure) Tia Maria
dash chocolate syrup
30 ml (1 measure) cream

Combine ice, Kahlua, crème de cacao, Baileys, Tia Maria, chocolate syrup and cream in blender; blend well. Pour into large goblet.

Mudslide

ice
30 ml (1 measure) Kahlua
30 ml (1 measure) Baileys
30 ml (1 measure) vodka

Place ice in tumbler. Pour over Kahlua, Baileys and vodka. Serve with a swizzle stick.

B52

30 ml (1 measure) Kahlua
30 ml (1 measure) Baileys
30 ml (1 measure) Cointreau

Pour Kahlua, then Baileys and finally Cointreau into a short liqueur or shot glass. Do not stir or mix. Ingredients should form three layers.

Robbie's Regret

ice
30 ml (1 measure) Kahlua
30 ml (1 measure)
    banana liqueur
15 ml (¹/₂ measure) light rum
90 ml (3 measures) cream
grated nutmeg

Place ice, Kahlua, banana liqueur, rum and cream in cocktail shaker: shake well. Strain into martini glass. Sprinkle with nutmeg.

Left to right: Heaven, B52, Robbie's Regret, Mudslide

TIA MARIA

Avalanche

ice
30 ml (1 measure) Tia Maria
30 ml (1 measure) Cointreau
45 ml (1½ measures)
    orange juice
30 ml (1 measure) cream

Combine ice, Tia Maria, Cointreau, orange juice and cream in cocktail shaker; shake well. Strain into champagne saucer.

Lazy Daze

ice
30 ml (1 measure) Tia Maria
15 ml (½ measure) vodka
30 ml (1 measure) green
    crème de menthe
lemonade
30 ml (1 measure) cream

Half fill a goblet with ice. Pour over Tia Maria, vodka and green crème de menthe; stir to mix. Top with lemonade; float cream on top.

Brown Cow

ice
30 ml (1 measure) Tia Maria
60 ml (2 measures) milk
ground cinnamon

Combine ice, Tia Maria and milk in cocktail shaker; shake well. Strain into martini glass. Sprinkle with cinnamon.

Sweet Maria

ice
30 ml (1 measure) Tia Maria
30 ml (1 measure) bourbon
30 ml (1 measure) cream
grated nutmeg

Combine ice, Tia Maria, bourbon and cream in cocktail shaker; shake well. Strain into martini glass. Sprinkle with nutmeg.

Lovers' Cocktail

ice
60 ml (2 measures)
    Tia Maria
30 ml (1 measure) tequila

Combine ice, Tia Maria and tequila in cocktail shaker; shake well. Strain into martini glass. Serve with a short straw.

Left to right: Lovers' Cocktail, Avalanche, Lazy Daze, Brown Cow, Sweet Maria

Toblerone

ice
30 ml (1 measure) Tia Maria
30 ml (1 measure) Frangelico
60 ml (2 measures) cream
1 teaspoon creamed honey

Combine ice, Tia Maria, Frangelico, cream and honey in cocktail shaker; shake well. Strain into large goblet.

Tia Fiesta

ice
30 ml (1 measure) Tia Maria
30 ml (1 measure) dark rum
30 ml (1 measure) tequila
30 ml (1 measure)
    pineapple juice
30 ml (1 measure)
    coconut cream

Combine ice, Tia Maria, dark rum, tequila, pineapple juice and coconut cream in cocktail shaker; shake well. Strain into a highball glass.

Left to right: Tia Fiesta, Toblerone, Screaming Lizard, Grasshopper

CREME DE MENTHE

This peppermint-flavoured liqueur comes in two forms, green and white. Both have the same taste.

Screaming Lizard

ice
30 ml (1 measure) green
   crème de menthe
30 ml (1 measure)
   green chartreuse
30 ml (1 measure)
   soda water

Place ice in tumbler. Add crème de menthe, green chartreuse and soda water; stir.

Grasshopper

ice
45 ml (1½ measures) green
   crème de menthe
30 ml (1 measure) white
   crème de cacao
60 ml (2 measures) cream

Place ice, crème de menthe, white crème de cacao and cream in a cocktail shaker; shake well. Strain into martini glass.

DRAMBUIE

The best known of liqueurs based on Scotch whisky, Drambuie is flavoured with herbs and rich heather honey.

Jungle Juice

crushed ice
30 ml (1 measure) Drambuie
30 ml (1 measure) light rum
30 ml (1 measure)
   coconut milk
30 ml (1 measure) cream
30 ml (1 measure)
   pineapple juice
1/2 banana, peeled and sliced

Combine ice, Drambuie, rum, coconut milk, cream, pineapple juice and banana in blender; blend well. Pour into highball glass. Serve with a straw.

The Jaffa

ice
30 ml (1 measure) Drambuie
15 ml (1/2 measure)
   Scotch whisky
15 ml (1/2 measure)
   crème de cacao
60 ml (2 measures)
   orange juice
30 ml (1 measure) cream

Combine ice, Drambuie, Scotch whisky, crème de cacao, orange juice and cream in cocktail shaker; shake well. Strain into highball glass.

Drambuie Snifter

60 ml (2 measures) Drambuie
30 ml (1 measure) cognac

Combine Drambuie and cognac in a warmed brandy balloon (see page 33).

Bobby Burns

ice
30 ml (1 measure) Drambuie
30 ml (1 measure)
   Scotch whisky
15 ml (1/2 measure)
   dry vermouth
15 ml (1/2 measure)
   sweet vermouth
dash Benedictine

Combine ice, Drambuie, whisky, vermouths and Benedictine in shaker; shake well. Strain into martini glass.

Drambuie Sour

ice
60 ml (2 measures) Drambuie
3 teaspoons lemon juice
1 teaspoon sugar
soda water

Combine ice, Drambuie, lemon juice and sugar in cocktail shaker; shake well. Strain into highball glass. Top with soda water.

Left to right: Drambuie Sour, The Jaffa, Bobby Burns, Drambuie Snifter, Jungle Juice

SCHNAPPS

This Northern European liqueur is made from potatoes—in times past it was often distilled at home and drunk to ward off icy Northern winters. These days, schnapps comes in more palatable varieties, and is often drunk, with other liqueurs, in the form of 'shooters' (see recipes below).

Sweet Tooth

ice
30 ml (1 measure)
    butterscotch schnapps
15 ml (¹/2 measure) Frangelico
15 ml (¹/2 measure)
    Vandermint
30 ml (1 measure) cream

Combine ice, schnapps, Frangelico, Vandermint and cream in shaker; shake well. Strain into goblet.

Cough Drop

30 ml (1 measure)
    butterscotch schnapps
15 ml (¹/2 measure) green
    crème de menthe

Pour schnapps, then green crème de menthe into shot glass, so that crème de menthe floats on top. (To be drunk all at once.)

Mint Slice

30 ml (1 measure)
    peppermint schnapps
15 ml (¹/2 measure) Kahlua

Pour schnapps, then Kahlua into shot glass. Serve ungarnished. (To be drunk all at once.)

Russian Front

ice
30 ml (1 measure)
    peach schnapps
30 ml (1 measure) vodka
30 ml (1 measure)
    raspberry cordial
champagne

Combine ice, peach schnapps, vodka and raspberry cordial in cocktail shaker; shake well. Strain into champagne flute. Top with champagne. Stir gently with a swizzle stick.

Barman's Breakfast

30 ml (1 measure)
    peach schnapps
15 ml (¹/2 measure) Advocaat

Pour schnapps, then Advocaat into shot glass, so that Advocaat floats on top. (To be drunk all at once.)

Left to right: Russian Front, Sweet Tooth, Cough Drop, Mint Slice, Barman's Breakfast

Shooting Star

30 ml (1 measure)
   butterscotch schnapps
15 ml (1/2 measure) Baileys

Pour butterscotch schnapps then Baileys into shot glass so that Baileys floats on top. (To be drunk all at once.)

Silk Stocking

ice
30 ml (1 measure)
   butterscotch schnapps
15 ml (1/2 measure) Advocaat
15 ml (1/2 measure)
   white crème de cacao
30 ml (1 measure) cream

Combine ice, schnapps, Advocaat, crème de cacao and cream in blender; blend well. Strain into a goblet.

Left to right: Nutty 'Nana, Silk Stocking, Shooting Star, Alex Special

FRANGELICO

This delicious hazelnut-flavoured liqueur blends well with bananas and creamy ingredients.

Nutty 'Nana

1 tablespoon chocolate syrup
crushed ice
30 ml (1 measure) Frangelico
30 ml (1 measure) brown
    crème de cacao
30 ml (1 measure)
    banana liqueur
30 ml (1 measure) cream

Drizzle chocolate syrup down the sides of a large goblet. Combine ice, Frangelico, crème de cacao, banana liqueur and cream in blender; blend well. Strain into goblet.

Alex Special

crushed ice
30 ml (1 measure) Frangelico
15 ml (1/2 measure) Tia Maria
15 ml (1/2 measure) Baileys
30 ml (1 measure) cream
banana, mashed

Place ice, Frangelico, Tia Maria, Baileys, cream and banana in blender; blend well. Pour into a large goblet.

PEACH LIQUEUR

Peach Surprise

ice
30 ml (1 measure)
    peach liqueur
30 ml (1 measure)
    banana liqueur
15 ml (1/2 measure) Malibu
3 teaspoons lemon juice
4 strawberries
dash grenadine

Combine ice, peach liqueur, banana liqueur, Malibu, lemon juice, strawberries and grenadine in blender; blend well. Pour into champagne flute.

Peach Haze

30 ml (1 measure)
    peach liqueur
30 ml (1 measure) peach
    purée
chilled champagne

Combine peach liqueur and peach puree in a champagne flute; stir. Top with champagne.

Fuzzy Peach

ice
30 ml (1 measure)
    peach liqueur
3 teaspoons Amaretto liqueur
2 scoops vanilla ice-cream
1 peach, peeled and chopped

Place ice, peach liqueur, Amaretto, ice-cream and peach in blender;

blend well. Pour into goblet. Serve with a straw.

Tropical Sunrise

ice
30 ml (1 measure)
    peach liqueur
30 ml (1 measure) Midori
15 ml (1/2 measure) vodka
30 ml (1 measure)
    coconut cream
30 ml (1 measure)
    orange juice
30 ml (1 measure)
    pineapple juice
1 teaspoon lemon juice

Place ice, peach liqueur, Midori, vodka, coconut cream, orange juice, pineapple juice and lemon juice in cocktail shaker; shake well. Strain into large goblet.

The Ripper

ice
30 ml (1 measure)
    peach liqueur
30 ml (1 measure)
    banana liqueur
30 ml (1 measure)
    dry vermouth
1 teaspoon blue curaçao
3 teaspoons lemon juice

Shake ice, peach liqueur, banana liqueur, vermouth, blue curaçao and lemon juice in cocktail shaker; shake well. Strain into goblet. Serve with a straw.

Left to right: The Ripper, Peach Surprise, Peach Haze, Fuzzy Peach, Tropical Sunrise

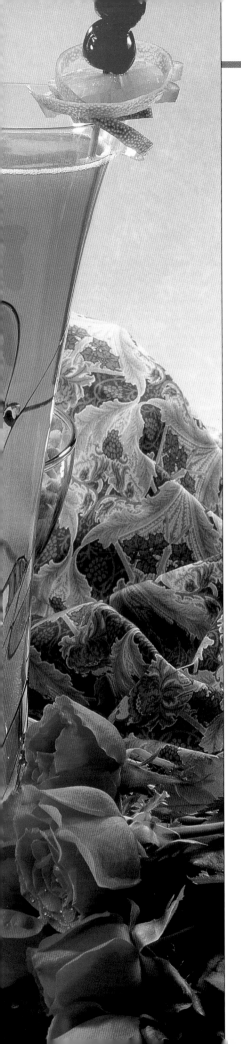

GRAPES & BUBBLES

CHAMPAGNE

Champagne is too volatile to be either shaken or stirred with ice. The champagne should be well chilled and poured slowly.

Ritz Fizz

dash blue curaçao
dash Amaretto
dash lemon juice
chilled champagne

Combine curaçao, Amaretto and lemon juice in a champagne flute; stir, then slowly top with champagne. Float some white rose petals on top, if desired.

Champagne Cocktail

sugar cube
dash bitters
15 ml ($^{1}/_{2}$ measure) brandy
chilled champagne

Place the sugar cube in a champagne flute. Add a dash of bitters, then brandy. Slowly top with champagne.

Buck's Fizz

120 ml (4 measures)
 orange juice, chilled
dash grenadine
chilled champagne

Pour orange juice and grenadine into champagne flute. Top slowly with champagne.

Black Velvet

The roasted malt in stout gives this popular drink its dark, almost bitter, flavour.

90 ml (3 measures)
 stout beer, chilled
90 ml (3 measures)
 chilled champagne

Pour beer, then champagne into champagne flute. Do not stir. Decorate with flowers, if desired.

Left to right: Ritz Fizz, Black Velvet, Champagne Cocktail, Buck's Fizz

French Kiss

15 ml (½ measure)
  raspberry liqueur
dash crème de cassis
chilled champagne
1 scoop ice-cream

Combine raspberry liqueur and crème de cassis in a champagne flute; stir to combine. Slowly top with champagne; float a scoop of ice-cream on top.

Champagne Cooler

30 ml (1 measure) brandy
30 ml (1 measure) Cointreau
2 dashes grenadine
dash bitters
chilled champagne

Combine brandy, Cointreau, grenadine and bitters in a champagne flute; stir to combine. Slowly top with champagne.

Left to right: French Kiss, Champagne Tory, Shampoo, Champagne Cooler

Shampoo

30 ml (1 measure) gin
15 ml (¹/₂ measure)
    lemon juice
dash Pernod
dash blue curaçao
chilled champagne

Combine gin, lemon juice, Pernod
and blue curaçao in a mixing jug;
stir to combine, then pour into a
champagne saucer. Top with
champagne.

Champagne Tory

15 ml (¹/₂ measure)
    banana liqueur
15 ml (¹/₂ measure)
    strawberry liqueur
15 ml (¹/₂ measure) Midori
chilled champagne

Combine   banana   liqueur,
strawberry liqueur and Midori in
a champagne flute; stir to
combine. Top with champagne.

Kir Royale

**2 dashes crème de cassis
chilled champagne**

Pour crème de cassis into champagne flute and slowly top with champagne.

Mango Bellini

**15 ml (¹/₂ measure)
 mango juice
chilled champagne**

Pour mango juice into champagne flute and slowly top with champagne.

Left to right: Mango Bellini, Kir, Kir Royale, Sangria

WINE

Sangria

This traditional Spanish drink can be made in large quantities, and its flavour will improve over several hours—it can be be made up to a day in advance. Seasonal fruits, such as peaches, pears and pineapples, can be added to this basic recipe. Good quality wine will be wasted in Sangria; use a table wine, even a cask wine.

**2 tablespoons caster
(superfine) sugar
15 ml ($\frac{1}{2}$ measure)
lemon juice
15 ml ($\frac{1}{2}$ measure)
orange juice
orange, thinly sliced
lemon, thinly sliced
lime, thinly sliced
ice
1 bottle red wine, chilled**

Mix sugar, lemon and orange juice in a large pitcher until sugar has dissolved. Add sliced fruit, wine and plenty of ice and stir well. Serve in large wine glasses. (Do not strain.)
Serves 6–8

Kir

**15 ml ($\frac{1}{2}$ measure)
crème de cassis
dry white wine, chilled**

Pour crème de cassis into large wine glass. Top with white wine.

VERMOUTH

Vermouth is a blend of white wines and strong herbs. Its two main types are dry and sweet.

Americano

ice
30 ml (1 measure)
    sweet vermouth
30 ml (1 measure) Campari
soda water

Combine ice, sweet vermouth and Campari in highball glass; stir to mix. Top with soda water. Serve with a swizzle stick.

San Martin

ice
45 ml (1¹/₂ measures)
    dry vermouth
45 ml (1¹/₂ measures)
    fino sherry
30 ml (1 measure) gin

Combine ice, dry vermouth, fino sherry and gin in cocktail shaker; shake well. Strain into a martini glass.

Victor Bravo

ice
30 ml (1 measure)
    sweet vermouth
30 ml (1 measure) brandy
30 ml (1 measure) gin

Combine ice, sweet vermouth, brandy and gin in shaker; shake well. Strain into martini glass.

Mr Whippy

ice
30 ml (1 measure)
    dry vermouth
30 ml (1 measure)
    Grand Marnier
orange-flavoured mineral
    water
dash grenadine
dash orange curaçao
15 ml (¹/₂ measure) cream

Half fill a large goblet with ice. Pour over dry vermouth and Grand Marnier; stir to combine. Top with orange-flavoured mineral water; add one dash each of grenadine and orange curaçao. Float cream on top by pouring slowly over the back of a spoon.

Grapefruit Aperitif

ice
30 ml (1 measure)
    dry vermouth
30 ml (1 measure)
    sweet vermouth
15 ml (¹/₂ measure)
    grapefruit juice
soda water

Half-fill a tumbler with ice. Pour over dry vermouth, sweet vermouth and grapefruit juice. Top with soda water.

Left to right: San Martin, Mr Whippy, Grapefruit Aperitif, Victor Bravo, Americano

SUMMER STUNNERS

PUNCHES

Punches are the perfect accompaniment to summer entertaining—use as many fruits as you like, and experiment with combinations of liquid ingredients. Non-alcoholic ingredients, such as fruit juices, can be frozen and added to the punch when needed. (This will help to keep it cool.)

Summer Wine Punch

6 cups peeled and chopped
   fresh fruit in season, such
   as strawberries, peaches,
   mangoes and pineapple
2 tablespoons caster
   (superfine) sugar
ice
1½ litres (8 cups) chilled
   medium-dry white wine
60 ml (2 measures) Cointreau
30 ml (1 measure)
   maraschino liqueur

Place 4–5 cups fruit in punch bowl; sprinkle with sugar; stand 1 hour. Cover fruit with enough ice to fill half the bowl. Pour over wine, Cointreau and maraschino liqueur; stir. Decorate with remaining fruit. (Punch will be very potent at first, but alcohol content will dilute as the ice melts.)
Serves 10–15

Midori Punch

ice
750 ml (3 cups) Midori
750 ml (3 cups) vodka
375 ml (1½ cups) lemonade
375 ml (1½ cups) soda water
honeydew melon balls
kiwi fruit slices
blood orange slices

Half-fill a punch bowl or jug with ice. Pour over Midori, vodka, lemonade and soda water; stir. Add honeydew melon balls, slices of kiwi fruit and orange slices.
Serves 15–20

Left to right: Summer Wine Punch, Midori Punch

Chocolate Punch

crushed ice
375 ml (1½ cups) Baileys
1 litre (4 cups) chilled milk
grated nutmeg

Combine ice, Baileys and milk in
blender; blend well. Strain into a
serving jug. Sprinkle with grated
nutmeg.
Serves 4

Lemon Daiquiri Punch

ice
375 ml (1½ cups) light rum
180 ml (6 measures)
    Cointreau
180 ml (6 measures) bottled
    lemon juice
750 ml (3 cups)
    lemon-flavoured mineral
    water
30 ml (1 measure) blue
    curaçao

Place ice in punch bowl. Add rum,
Cointreau, lemon juice, flavoured
mineral water and blue curaçao.
Stir to mix. If punch proves too
tart, add a tablespoon of caster
(superfine) sugar or serve punch in
sugar-frosted punch cups.
Serves 8–10

*Left to right: Pimm's Punch,
Chocolate Punch, Lemon
Daiquiri Punch*

Pimm's Punch

ice
375 ml (1 1/2 cups)
    Pimm's No. 1
375 ml (1 1/2 cups) bourbon
180 ml (6 measures)
    sweet vermouth
180 ml (6 measures)
    light rum
300 ml (10 1/2 fl oz)
    orange juice
750 ml (3 cups) champagne
a selection of chopped or
    sliced fresh fruit in
    season, such as star fruit,
    kiwi fruit, pawpaw,
    pineapple, strawberries,
    cherries
75 ml (1/3 cup) orange juice,
    extra, frozen in ice-cube
    tray

Place ice in punch bowl. Add
Pimm's, bourbon, vermouth and
rum; stir to mix. Pour in orange
juice and champagne. Add fruit
and frozen cubes of orange juice.
Serve immediately.
Serves 10–12

NON-ALCOHOLIC DRINKS

Black Widow Spider

crushed ice
cola
1 scoop vanilla ice-cream
whipped cream

Place ice in highball glass. Add cola until two-thirds full and carefully add a scoop of ice-cream. Do not stir. Top with cream. Serve with straws and a parfait spoon.

Shirley Temple

crushed ice
good dash grenadine
lemonade
30 ml (1 measure) cream

Place ice in highball glass. Add grenadine and top with lemonade. Use the back of a teaspoon to slowly float the cream over the lemonade. Serve with a straw.

Homemade Lemonade

Lemon Syrup
6 large lemons
6 whole cloves
boiling water
460 g (2 cups) sugar

ice
soda water

To make Lemon Syrup:
Slice 6 lemons; place in a large bowl with the cloves and cover with boiling water. Leave to infuse overnight. Strain water into a large pan; discard lemon slices and cloves. Add sugar to pan; stir, without boiling, until sugar dissolves, then bring to boil and simmer for 10 minutes until liquid is thick and syrupy. Cool.
To serve Lemonade:
Place ice in highball glass. Pourover 30 ml (1 measure) of lemon syrup and top with soda water.

Left to right: Black Widow Spider, Homemade Lemonade, Shirley Temple

Virgin Mary

2 teaspoons celery salt
1 teaspoon black pepper
ice
120 ml (4 measures)
    tomato juice
15 ml (¹/₂ measure)
    lemon juice
2 dashes worcestershire
    sauce
dash Tabasco sauce

Frost the rim of a large goblet with combined celery salt and pepper (see page 5). Combine ice, tomato juice, lemon juice, worcestershire sauce and Tabasco sauce in cocktail shaker; shake well. Strain into goblet.

Iced Tea

ice
120 ml (4 measures) cold
    black tea
1 teaspoon sugar

Place ice, cold tea and sugar in highball glass; stir with a swizzle stick.

Variation: Iced Tea can also be made with cold herbal teas.

Limeade

ice
juice of 3 limes
30 ml (1 measure)
    sugar syrup
soda water
dash bitters

Combine ice, lime juice and syrup in a highball glass. Top with soda water and a dash of bitters.

Boo Boo's Special

ice
90 ml (3 measures)
    pineapple juice
90 ml (3 measures)
    orange juice
dash bitters
dash grenadine

Combine ice, pineapple juice, orange juice and bitters in cocktail shaker; shake well. Strain into large goblet. Add dash of grenadine. Serve with a straw.

Left to right: Iced Tea, Boo Boo's Special, Virgin Mary, Limeade

AFTER MIDNIGHT
WARMING DRINKS

After Dinner Mint

1 heaped teaspoon cocoa
   powder or drinking
   chocolate
boiling water
30 ml (1 measure)
   peppermint schnapps
   (or crème de menthe)
whipped cream

Make up the cocoa by combining cocoa powder and boiling water in a liqueur coffee glass. Add schnapps and stir. Spoon or pipe whipped cream on top.

Mexican Coffee

30 ml (1 measure) tequila
15 ml (¹/₂ measure) Kahlua
120 ml (4 measures)
   strong black coffee
whipped cream
cocoa powder

Pour tequila and Kahlua into liqueur coffee glass. Top with coffee and stir. Gently spoon or pipe whipped cream on surface. Sprinkle with cocoa powder.

Jamaican Coffee

30 ml (1 measure) Tia Maria
15 ml (¹/₂ measure) dark rum
120 ml (4 measures) strong
   black coffee
whipped cream

Pour Tia Maria and rum into liqueur coffee glass. Top with coffee and stir. Gently spoon or pipe dollops of whipped cream on surface.

Irish Coffee

1 teaspoon soft brown sugar
30 ml (1 measure)
   Irish whiskey
120 ml (4 measures)
   strong black coffee
whipped cream
grated nutmeg

Combine sugar and whiskey in a liqueur coffee glass. Top with coffee and stir. Gently spoon whipped cream on surface. Sprinkle with grated nutmeg.

Left to right: Irish Coffee, Jamaican Coffee, Mexican Coffee, After Dinner Mint

NIGHTCAPS

Gluhwein

1 cinnamon stick
6 cloves
6 allspice berries
750 ml (3 cups) red wine
30 ml (1 measure) port
1 tablespoon sugar
lemon, thinly sliced

Combine cinnamon, cloves, allspice berries, wine, port, sugar and lemon in a heavy-based pan. Heat without boiling. Serve warm; do not strain.
Serves 4–6

P.S. I Love You

ice
30 ml (1 measure) Amaretto
30 ml (1 measure) Kahlua
30 ml (1 measure) Baileys
grated nutmeg

Half fill a tumbler with ice; add Amaretto, Kahlua, then Baileys. Stir with a swizzle stick; sprinkle nutmeg on top.

Hot Buttered Rum

1 teaspoon butter
1 teaspoon soft brown sugar
dash rum essence
cinnamon
45 ml (1½ measures)
    dark rum
boiling water

Mix softened butter with sugar, essence and cinnamon until well combined. Place butter mixture in large, warmed goblet and add rum, then boiling water. Stir well to combine and serve immediately.

Hot Toddy

60 ml (2 measures) Scotch
    whisky (or preferred spirit
    or liqueur)
1 teaspoon honey or soft
    brown sugar
boiling water
slice of lemon studded with
    cloves
cinnamon stick

Pour whisky into large, warmed goblet, add honey or sugar and top with boiling water. Add lemon slice and cinnamon stick and stir gently.

Left to right: Hot Buttered Rum, Hot Toddy, P.S. I Love You, Gluhwein

THE MORNING AFTER

Alcohol dehydrates the body and saps vitamins, especially B, and minerals from your system—which is why you wake up feeling thirsty and listless after too much of a good thing. Drink as much water as you can before going to bed, however if you need a quick pick-me-up the next day, here are some ways of restoring lost fluids and nutrients.

Fernet Branca

ice
45 ml (1½ measures)
 Fernet Branca
45 ml (1½ measures) Pernod

Mix ice, Fernet Branca and Pernod in a tumbler; swallow in one gulp.

Prairie Oyster

1 tablespoon worcestershire
 sauce
2 drops Tabasco sauce
egg yolk
good dash salt and pepper

Combine worcestershire sauce, Tabasco sauce, egg yolk, salt and pepper in shot glass; swallow in one gulp. (Followed by a beer chaser, this is known as a Bush Oyster.)

Bullshot

ice
30 ml (1 measure) vodka
125 ml (½ cup) beef stock
1 teaspoon lemon juice
dash worcestershire sauce
good dash salt and pepper

Combine ice, vodka, beef stock, lemon juice, worcestershire sauce, salt and pepper in a cocktail shaker; shake well. Strain into a highball glass.

Quick Fixes

• **Underberg:** 30 ml (1 measure) Underberg in a shot glass.
• **Boilermaker:** 30 ml (1 measure) Scotch whisky in shot glass followed by a 250 ml (1 cup) beer chaser.
• **Claytons Cure:** Top 30 ml (1 measure) Claytons Tonic with soda water.
• **Red Eye:** Combine 250 ml (1 cup) beer with 60 ml (2 measures) tomato juice in a beer glass.
• **Cinderella:** Combine 125 ml (½ cup) orange juice, 125 ml (½ cup) pineapple juice and 30 ml (1 measure) lemon juice in a large goblet.
• **Black coffee**

If All Else Fails...

2 soluble vitamin B tablets
1 glass water
12 hours sleep

Dissolve tablets in water; swallow then take sleep.

Top row (left to right): Boilermaker, Vitamin B tablets, Fernet Branca, Underberg, Black Coffee; Bottom row (left to right): Red Eye, Prairie Oyster, Cinderella, Claytons Cure, Bullshot

GLOSSARY

Advocaat: Dutch liqueur, yellow in colour, made from brandy, egg yolks and neutral spirits. Very sweet and thick.

Amaretto: Italian liqueur flavoured with almonds and apricot kernels.

aperitif: a drink consumed before a meal to stimulate the appetite.

Benedictine: amber-coloured French liqueur based on brandy and flavoured with herbs.

bitters: a range of spirits flavoured with aromatic and bitter herbs drunk (diluted) as an aperitif or, more often, used as a flavouring in mixed drinks.

celery salt: mild vegetable salt used for frosting glasses or seasoning savoury drinks.

chartreuse: French liqueur flavoured with over 130 spices and herbs; available in green or yellow varieties. It is highly pungent in taste and aroma.

chaser: a drink of water, beer or other mild beverage taken after a drink of spirits.

cherry liqueur: brandy-based liqueur flavoured with dark cherries. Also known as cherry brandy.

Claytons Tonic: non-alcoholic cola-style mixer.

coconut cream: thick liquid, made from pressing coconut flesh, used to flavour many drinks.

cognac: a high quality brandy.

cordial: sweet, non-alcoholic essence made from fruit and mixed with water or other liquids; available in lime, lemon, orange, raspberry and others.

crème de banane: brandy-based, pale-yellow liqueur flavoured with banana.

crème de cacao: liqueur flavoured with roasted cocoa beans and vanilla; available in white or brown varieties.

crème de cassis: dark-red liqueur flavoured with blackcurrants.

crème de fraises: strawberry flavoured liqueur.

curaçao: generic term for any spirit-based liqueur flavoured with oranges; available in white, orange, blue or green varieties. It was originally made on the island of Curaçao.

dash: a very small quantity, roughly equivalent to $1/6$ teaspoon.

egg white: (as used in cocktails) a small amount is beaten or shaken to provide froth and bulk in a drink.

Fernet Branca: Italian bitters drunk as an aperitif or pick-me-up.

fino sherry: a very dry sherry.

green ginger wine: wine flavoured with fruit and ginger.

grenadine: non-alcoholic red cordial used for sweetness and colour.

liqueur: any spirit which has been sweetened and flavoured, most typically with fruit, herbs or nuts.

maraschino cherry: a cherry cooked in sugar and imitation maraschino liqueur.

maraschino liqueur: colourless Italian liqueur flavoured with wild cherries, known as marascas.

measure: cup which contains 30 ml (1 fl oz) and is used to mix cocktails.

neat: a drink of undiluted alcohol.

nightcap: alcoholic drink taken before sleep; often a hot or warmed drink.

Parfait Amour: light purple French liqueur flavoured with herbs and citrus fruit.

Pernod: colourless spirit flavoured with aniseed; often drunk as an aperitif.

shot glass: small glass in which shooters are served.

shooter: short drink of only alcoholic ingredients, served ungarnished and at room temperature, and intended to be drunk all at once.

spirit: any distilled alcoholic liquor such as brandy, gin or whisky.

sugar: (as used in cocktails) a sweetener often made up into sugar syrup, although demerara sugar and caster (superfine) sugar can be added directly to drinks; also used for frosting glasses.

toddy: mixture of alcohol, flavourings and hot water.

triple sec: another term for white curaçao.

Underberg: German digestive bitters taken as a pick-me-up.

Vandermint: Dutch liqueur flavoured with mint and chocolate.

vermouth: a wine fortified with herbs.

INDEX

This edition published in 2006 by Bay Books, an imprint of Murdoch Books Pty Limited,
Pier 8/9, 23 Hickson Road, Millers Point, NSW 2000, Australia.

Editorial Director: Rachel Carter **Editor:** Amanda Bishop
Creative Director: Marylouise Brammer
Designer: Jackie Richards **Design Assistant:** Southida Vongsaphay
Food Director: Lulu Grimes **Food Editor:** Kerrie ray
Barman/Cocktail Consultant: Robbie Mau
Photographer: Peter Scott **Step Photography:** Reg Morrison
Food Stylist: Rosemary De Santis
Home Economist: Dimitra Stais
Chief Executive: Juliet Rogers **Publisher:** Kay Scarlett

ISBN 1-74045-930-X
Printed by Sing Cheong Printing Co. Ltd. Printed in China.